The

Time

Manager

Table of Content

INTRODUCTION

The most valuable resource you have as an entrepreneur is time. Managing your company and team, keeping up with market trends, and networking with new customers and partners are just a few of the numerous demands on your time that you must deal with every day. In today's fast-paced business world, effective time management is crucial for success.

But many business owners find it difficult to adequately manage their time. Burnout, stress, and a sense of overwhelm are all common side effects of the responsibilities of running a business. That's why this book is here to help.

The essential methods and tools for efficient time management as an entrepreneur are covered in this book. Regardless of your level of experience as a business owner, you'll learn methods for setting priorities, using your time effectively, and striking a healthy work-life balance.

You'll find useful tips, practical examples, and suggestions that you can use right away in your own business throughout the whole book. You'll learn how to set priorities, evaluate your time, and manage your time more efficiently using tools and strategies like time blocking, scheduling, and delegating.

You'll also learn techniques for overcoming typical time management difficulties like procrastination and communication overload, as well as long-term maintenance plans for your time management system.

By the time you finish reading this book, you'll have a thorough understanding of the significance of time management for entrepreneurs as well as the skills and strategies required to efficiently manage your time and accomplish your professional objectives.

The Importance of Time Management for Entrepreneurs

For a number of reasons, effective time management is essential for business owners. Here are some of the most important:

Increasing productivity: Entrepreneurs often juggle several responsibilities and wear many hats. Making the most of their time and energy through effective time management boosts productivity and enables business owners to do more tasks in less time.

Meeting deadlines: You probably have a lot of deadlines as an entrepreneur, from client deliverables to business development objectives. You can guarantee that you achieve these dates and prevent the stress and drawbacks of missing deadlines by carefully managing your time.

Achieving work-life balance: Entrepreneurship can be all-consuming, and it's easy to let work take over your personal life. Effective time management allows you to prioritize your work responsibilities while also making time for personal activities, hobbies, and relationships. This can help you avoid burnout and maintain your overall well-being.

Making better decisions: When you're rushing to complete tasks and constantly feeling overwhelmed, it's easy to make mistakes or overlook important details. Effective time management allows you to take a step back, evaluate your priorities, and make better decisions based on a clear understanding of your goals and available resources.

Building a successful business: Ultimately, effective time management is essential for building a successful business. By managing your time effectively, you can focus on the most important tasks that will move your business forward, while avoiding distractions and time-wasters that can detract from your success.

What you'll learn in this book

Welcome to "Time Management for Entrepreneurs"! This book is designed to provide you with the necessary tools and techniques to help you manage your time effectively and become a more productive entrepreneur.

In this book, you will learn:

- The importance of time management for entrepreneurs: In this book, we will discuss why time management is crucial for entrepreneurs and how it can impact your success.

- How to set clear goals and prioritize tasks: Setting clear goals and prioritizing tasks is essential for effective time management. You will learn how to set SMART goals and prioritize your tasks based on their importance and urgency.

- Strategies for managing your time: There are many strategies and techniques for managing your time effectively. In this book, we will discuss some of the most effective strategies, including the Pomodoro Technique, time blocking, and batching.

- Tips for avoiding distractions: As an entrepreneur, it's easy to get distracted by emails, phone calls, and social media notifications. You will learn some tips and techniques for avoiding distractions and staying focused on your goals.

- Time-saving tools and apps: There are many time-saving tools and apps that can help you manage your time more effectively. We will introduce you to some of the best tools and apps for managing your schedule, delegating tasks, and tracking your time.

- Strategies for delegating tasks: Delegating tasks is an essential part of time management. You will learn how to delegate tasks effectively, including how to choose the right person for the job and how to communicate your expectations clearly.

- How to make time for self-care: As an entrepreneur, it's easy to get caught up in your work and neglect your own well-being. We will discuss the importance of self-care and provide you with some tips and techniques for making time for self-care.

By the end of this book, you will have a comprehensive understanding of time management strategies and techniques that will help you become a more productive and successful entrepreneur. So, let's get started!

CHAPTER 1

Understanding Your Priorities: The Key to Effective Time Management

Being successful in life requires good time management because it is one of our most significant resources. When there are so many things demanding for your attention, it can be difficult to manage your time properly. Your ability to prioritize comes into play in this situation. You may make the most of your time and work more effectively toward your objectives by deciding which tasks are most crucial and concentrating your time and effort there.

Defining Your Priorities

Identifying what matters most to you personally is the first step in understanding your priorities. This may entail pausing to consider your objectives and morals. What are the things in life that are most important to you? What are your long-term goals? You may begin to identify the tasks and activities that will enable you to accomplish your priorities after you have a firm understanding of them.

You could find it useful to make a list of your goals and divide them into more manageable, doable tasks in order to choose your priorities. This might assist you in determining the precise actions that are necessary to achieving your goals. You might also want to think about what happens if you don't do some duties. Do some tasks require more urgency than others or have a bigger effect on your success as a whole?

Managing Your Priorities

Having determined your priorities, the next step is to manage them effectively. To do this, you might set clear goals and deadlines for yourself and divide more difficult tasks into more digestible chunks of subtasks. To make time for more important activities, you might also want to think about delegating tasks to others or outsourcing some of your task.

Learning to say no is a crucial part of prioritizing your tasks. Even while it may be tempting, saying yes to every opportunity that presents itself can rapidly result in overwhelm and burnout. Instead, concentrate on saying "yes" to possibilities that mesh with your priorities and "no" to opportunities that don't.

Understanding your priorities is key to effective time management. By identifying your most important tasks and focusing your time and energy on them, you can make the most of your time and achieve your goals more efficiently. The key is to be intentional and strategic about how you manage your time, with the right approach, you can achieve greater success in all areas of your life.

Identifying Your Most Important Tasks

In our busy lives, it can be easy to get caught up in the urgent tasks that demand our attention right now, and forget about the truly important tasks that will make the most difference in the long run. But by identifying your most important tasks, you can focus your time and energy where it matters most, and achieve your goals with greater efficiency and effectiveness.

Here are some tips for identifying your most important tasks:

1. Determine your goals

The first step in identifying your most important tasks is to determine your goals. What do you want to achieve in the short term and long term? What are your priorities? By clarifying your goals, you can identify the tasks that are most critical to achieving them.

2. Prioritize your tasks

Once you have determined your goals, you can prioritize your tasks based on their importance. Make a list of all the tasks you need to accomplish, and rank them in order of importance. Focus on the tasks at the top of your list first, as they will have the greatest impact on achieving your goals.

3. Consider the consequences

When prioritizing your tasks, consider the consequences of not completing them. What will happen if you don't complete a particular task? Will it have a significant impact on your goals or your life in general? By considering the consequences of not completing a task, you can better prioritize it among your other tasks.

4. Identify time-sensitive tasks

Some tasks are time-sensitive and require immediate attention. Identify these tasks and prioritize them accordingly. However, be careful not to let time-sensitive tasks distract you from the truly important tasks that will have a greater impact on achieving your goals.

5. Focus on your strengths

Identify the tasks that play to your strengths and prioritize them accordingly. By focusing on your strengths, you can accomplish tasks more quickly and effectively, and achieve your goals with greater ease.

6. Be flexible

Remember that priorities can shift as circumstances change. Be flexible and willing to adjust your priorities as needed. Don't be afraid to re-evaluate your list of tasks on a regular basis and make changes as necessary.

Identifying your most important tasks is essential to achieving your goals and living a fulfilling life. By clarifying your goals, prioritizing your tasks, considering the consequences, identifying time-sensitive tasks, focusing on your strengths, and being flexible, you can achieve your goals with greater efficiency and effectiveness. So take the time to identify your most important tasks, and make them a priority in your life.

Defining Your Long-Term Goals

Setting long-term goals is an essential step towards achieving success in both personal and professional aspects of life. These goals act as a roadmap, guiding individuals towards their desired destination. However, defining long-term goals can be a challenging task for many people, as it requires careful planning, introspection, and commitment.

We will explore the process of defining your long-term goals, including the benefits of having them, and some practical tips to help you set and achieve them.

Benefits of Having Long-Term Goals:

Having long-term goals provides several benefits that can help individuals lead a more purposeful and fulfilling life. Some of the key benefits are:

1. Direction: Long-term goals provide clarity and direction to individuals, helping them stay focused on their priorities and make informed decisions.

2. Motivation: Setting long-term goals gives individuals a sense of purpose and motivation to work towards something meaningful, which can help them overcome challenges and setbacks.

3. Self-Discovery: Defining long-term goals requires introspection and self-reflection, which can help individuals discover their true passions and values.

4. Growth: Pursuing long-term goals can help individuals develop new skills and knowledge, leading to personal and professional growth.

Steps to Define Long-Term Goals:

1. Identify your passions and values: The first step in defining long-term goals is to identify your passions and values. This will help you determine what matters most to you and what you want to achieve in life.

2. Determine your vision: Once you have identified your passions and values, determine your vision for the future. What do you want to accomplish in the long run? What kind of life do you want to lead? Answering these questions can help you create a vision that aligns with your passions and values.

3. Create SMART goals: SMART goals are specific, measurable, achievable, relevant, and time-bound. Creating SMART goals can help you break down your vision into smaller, manageable steps that you can work towards.

4. Develop a plan: Once you have created SMART goals, develop a plan to achieve them. This plan should include actionable steps, timelines, and resources required to achieve each goal.

5. Track your progress: Tracking your progress is essential to ensure that you stay on track and make progress towards your long-term goals. Regularly reviewing your progress can also help you make adjustments and course-correct if needed.

Tips for Achieving Long-Term Goals:

1. Stay focused: To achieve long-term goals, it's essential to stay focused on your priorities and avoid distractions.

2. Stay motivated: Motivation is key to achieving long-term goals. Celebrate small victories along the way to keep yourself motivated.

3. Stay committed: Achieving long-term goals requires commitment and perseverance. Stay committed to your goals, even when faced with setbacks or challenges.

4. Seek support: Seek support from friends, family, or mentors who can provide guidance, motivation, and accountability.

Conclusion:

Defining your long-term goals is an essential step towards achieving success and leading a fulfilling life. By identifying your passions, values, and vision, creating SMART goals, developing a plan, tracking your progress, and staying focused, motivated, and committed, you can achieve your long-term goals and create the life you want.

Creating a Mission Statement

For entrepreneurs to succeed in their commercial endeavors, effective time management is essential. Having a clear sense of purpose and direction is one of the key elements of effective time management. This is where a mission statement comes in.

A mission statement is a brief statement that sums up the core values of a business. Along with outlining the organization's aims and objectives, it also describes its mission and core values. In other words, a mission statement aids in outlining a company's goals and the purpose for its existence.

The value of establishing a mission statement is underlined. Without a strong sense of purpose, business, owners risk being weighed down in the day-to-day activities of running their business and never truly knowing if they are on the right track.

Consider your personal passions when you begin to build a mission statement for your business. What inspires you to wake up early and put in a lot of effort every day? What values are important to you, and how do they relate to your business?

Then, think about what you want your business to accomplish. What are your long-term objectives, and how do they relate to your core values? How can your business assist you in making the impact you desire to have on the world?

It's time to start writing your mission statement once you are certain of your purpose and objectives. Remember that your mission statement ought to be brief and simple to grasp. It should only contain a few phrases and should express the essence of what your business does. Use motivational and inspiring words when creating your mission statement. Make sure your statement is in line with your fundamental principles and use language that portrays a sense of purpose and passion.

Share your mission statement with others once it has been written. Make sure that everyone on your team is dedicated to working toward attaining the company's purpose and that they are aware of it. Everyone who works for you should be striving toward the same aims and objectives, and your mission statement should serve as a beacon for your business.

A mission statement should be written by every entrepreneur who is serious about success. You can make sure that you stay focused and motivated while you strive to create your business by taking the time to clarify your purpose and goals and creating a mission statement that encapsulates it. Your ability to maximize your time and accomplish your objectives will improve once you have a clear mission statement in place.

CHAPTER 2

Analyzing Your Time

Time management is essential for managing a business. Entrepreneurs frequently have limited resources, particularly time, and they must juggle a variety of jobs and responsibilities. Because of this, anyone who wants to be a successful entrepreneur must have the ability to analyze their time effectively.

One of the most popular time management books for entrepreneurs is "The 4-Hour Work Week" by Timothy Ferriss, in this book, Ferriss questions the conventional 9-to-5 workday and exhorts readers to place more emphasis on output than on the number of hours put in. He also emphasizes the importance of time analysis to find areas where you can be more effective and save time.

The 80/20 rule, commonly referred to as the Pareto Principle, is one of the main ideas in "The 4-Hour Work Week". According to this rule, only 20% of your efforts will provide 80% of your results. When it comes to time management, this implies that you should concentrate on the 20% of tasks that have the biggest impact on your business.

Start by deciding which of your duties are the most important before applying the 80/20 rule to your time management. These are the activities that have the most influence on your business, such as those that help you attract new clients or generate income. Once you've identified these activities, give them top priority over less important ones and concentrate on finishing them first.

Another principle in "The 4-Hour Work Week" is outsourcing. Ferriss encourages entrepreneurs to outsource tasks that are not their core competencies or that can be done more efficiently by someone else. For example, if you're not skilled at social media marketing, you could outsource this task to a freelancer or agency.

When analyzing your time, consider which tasks you could outsource to save time and be more efficient. This could include administrative tasks like bookkeeping or data entry, or more specialized tasks like graphic design or web development.

Finally, "The 4-Hour Work Week" emphasizes the importance of taking breaks and disconnecting from work. Ferriss argues that productivity and creativity suffer when we work too much and don't take time to recharge. By taking regular breaks and disconnecting from work, entrepreneurs can come back refreshed and energized, ready to tackle their most critical tasks.

Tracking Your Time

The first step in developing your time management abilities is tracking your time. You can spot places where improvements and adjustments can be made to help you use your time more efficiently by analyzing how you spend your time.

It's important to keep note of all of your activities, including work-related duties, leisure pursuits, and even downtime, before you begin tracking your time. Your activities and the time you spend on them can be recorded using a notebook, a spreadsheet, or a time-tracking app. To gain a clear picture of your daily routines and behaviors, make sure you track your time consistently for at least a week or two.

Once you have your time tracking data, you can analyze it to identify patterns and trends. Look for areas where you're spending too much or too little time and identify tasks that take up most of your time. For instance, you might find that you spend a lot of time on email or social media, which could be detracting from more important tasks.

With this information, you can start making changes to improve your time management skills. For instance, if you find that you're spending too much time on non-work-related activities, consider scheduling your downtime or leisure activities so that they don't interfere with your work. Or if you find that you're spending too much time on email or social media, you could set specific times during the day to check your inbox or log in to your social media accounts.

Review your time record and evaluate your results after keeping track of your time for a few days or a week. Examine your time usage for patterns and trends, such as the times of day when you are most productive and the times when you are most prone to distraction. You can use this information to develop a strategy for increased productivity and time management.

A crucial component of efficient time management for business owners is time tracking. You may find areas for improvement and implement adjustments to increase productivity and reach your goals by keeping a time log and reviewing your outcomes.

Identifying Time Wasters

Effective time management for entrepreneurs begins with identifying time wasters. Activities or routines that take up your time but don't add much value or advance your goals are known as time wasters. You may enhance your productivity and free up more time by figuring out where your time is being wasted and getting rid of it.

Here are some common time wasters to look out for:

1. Distractions: Distractions can come in many forms, such as social media notifications, emails, phone calls, or interruptions from coworkers. To avoid distractions, try setting aside specific times to check your email and social media accounts, and communicate with coworkers when you need uninterrupted time to focus on a task.

2. Procrastination: Procrastination is a common time waster that can prevent you from making progress on your goals. To avoid procrastination, try breaking your tasks down into smaller, more manageable steps, and set specific deadlines for each step.

3. Multitasking: Multitasking can seem like an efficient use of time, but it can actually decrease your productivity by dividing your focus and attention. Instead of multitasking,

try focusing on one task at a time and completing it before moving on to the next.

4. Meetings: Meetings can be a significant time drain, especially if they are not well-planned or focused. To make the most of your meeting time, try setting clear objectives and agendas, and limit the number of attendees to those who are essential to the discussion.

5. Procedural tasks: Procedural tasks are repetitive tasks that can be automated or delegated. By identifying these tasks and finding ways to streamline or delegate them, you can free up more time to focus on higher-value tasks.

To identify your own time wasters, try keeping a time log for a few days or a week, and then review your results to see where you are spending your time. Look for patterns and trends in your time usage, and ask yourself whether each activity is truly necessary or providing value. Once you have identified your time wasters, make a plan to eliminate or minimize them, and focus on the tasks and activities that will help you achieve your goals.

Setting Time Management Goals

In today's fast-paced world, where there are numerous distractions and conflicting demands on our attention, time management is essential. Effective time management can help you accomplish your goals and lessen stress whether you're a student, employee, or self-employed person. Setting time management objectives, however, might be difficult, especially if you're not used to scheduling your time. Here are some pointers for creating time management objectives that actually work:

- Identify your priorities: The first step in setting time management goals is to identify your priorities. This could be anything from completing a project for work, studying for an exam, or spending quality time with family and friends. Once you've identified your priorities, determine what you need to accomplish and when you need to complete them. Be specific and realistic about your priorities.

- Set SMART goals: SMART goals are Specific, Measurable, Achievable, Relevant, and Time-bound. Setting SMART goals will help you stay focused, motivated, and accountable. Make sure your goals are clear, quantifiable, and challenging but not impossible.

- Break down larger goals into smaller ones: If your goal is a large project or task, break it down into smaller, more manageable steps. This will help you make progress towards your goal without feeling overwhelmed. For example, if your goal is to write a research paper, break it down into smaller steps such as researching, outlining, writing the introduction, writing the body, and writing the conclusion.

- Use a planner or calendar: Use a planner or calendar to organize your time and keep track of your goals. Write down your goals, deadlines, and to-do lists to help you stay on track. This will help you see what needs to be done and when, and it will also help you avoid overbooking yourself.

- Prioritize your tasks: Prioritize your tasks based on their importance and urgency. This will help you focus on the most critical tasks and avoid wasting time on less important ones. Use the Eisenhower matrix to prioritize your tasks by classifying them as urgent and important, not urgent but important, urgent but not important, and not urgent or important. This will help you decide which tasks to tackle first.

- Set realistic deadlines: Set deadlines for each task or goals that are challenging but achievable. This will help you stay motivated and focused, while also avoiding procrastination.

Make sure you give yourself enough time to complete each task or goal, and be prepared to adjust your deadlines if necessary.

- Review your progress regularly: Regularly review your progress towards your goals to ensure that you're making progress and staying on track. If you're not meeting your goals, adjust your plan accordingly. This could mean re-prioritizing your tasks, adjusting your deadlines, or seeking help from others.

Setting time management goals is an essential step towards achieving your objectives and reducing stress. By following these tips, you can improve your productivity, stay focused and motivated, and achieve your goals in a timely and effective manner. Remember that time management is a skill that takes practice, so don't be discouraged if it takes time to get used to it. With practice, you can develop effective time management habits that will help you succeed in all areas of your life.

CHAPTER 3

Tools and Techniques for Time Management

The ability to manage our time well is crucial for attaining our goals and leading balanced lives. Because there are so many demands on our time and attention, it's simple to become overwhelmed and forget what's most important. We may successfully manage our time by using a variety of tools and strategies, which is fortunate. These methods and technologies can aid in task prioritization, distraction avoidance, and time efficiency. To-do lists, time blocking, the Pomodoro Technique, the Eisenhower Matrix, time tracking, batch processing, and delegation are some of the most well-liked time management tools and methods that will be covered. By becoming proficient with these tools and methods, we may increase our output, lessen our stress levels, and accomplish our goals.

- To-Do Lists: To-do lists are one of the most basic and effective tools for managing our time. A to-do list is a simple list of tasks that need to be completed. It can be created using pen and paper or through digital applications. A to-do list helps us prioritize our tasks, visualize what we need to accomplish, and reduce anxiety by breaking down large tasks into smaller, more manageable ones. Moreover, it helps us stay organized, avoid procrastination, and track our progress.

- Time Blocking: Time blocking is a time management technique that involves scheduling blocks of time for specific tasks. It helps us focus on one task at a time and avoid multitasking, which can be counterproductive. To use time blocking, we need to identify the tasks we need to complete and allocate specific blocks of time to work on each one. Time blocking can be done using digital calendars, or it can be done using a paper planner. By breaking our day into smaller, more manageable time blocks, we can accomplish more and feel less overwhelmed.

- The Pomodoro Technique: The Pomodoro Technique is a time management technique that involves breaking down work into intervals of 25 minutes, followed by a short break. This technique helps us stay focused and avoid burnout by providing regular breaks. The Pomodoro Technique can be implemented using apps. By focusing on one task at a time, we can increase our productivity and reduce stress.

- Eisenhower Matrix: The Eisenhower Matrix is a time management tool that helps us prioritize tasks by categorizing them based on urgency and importance. This technique helps us focus on the most critical tasks and avoid wasting time on less important ones. The Eisenhower Matrix can be created using digital tools. By prioritizing our tasks, we can make sure that we are focusing on the most important things first and using our time more effectively.

- Time Tracking: Time tracking involves monitoring the time we spend on tasks to identify where we can improve our time management. There are many time tracking apps available, these apps help us understand how we are spending our time, and they provide insights into how we can be more productive. By tracking our time, we can identify time-wasting activities and make adjustments to our schedule.

- Batch Processing: Batch processing involves grouping similar tasks together and completing them in one batch. This technique helps us avoid switching between different types of tasks and saves time. For example, we can batch process emails, phone calls, or paperwork. By completing similar tasks in one batch, we can reduce distractions and maintain focus.

- Delegation: Delegation involves assigning tasks to others who are better suited to complete them. This technique helps us free up time and focus on tasks that are more important or require our unique skills. Delegation can be done in the workplace or at home, and it requires good communication and trust. By delegating tasks to others, we can reduce our workload, reduce stress, and achieve more.

Everyone should learn time management skills to boost their productivity and effectiveness. The tools and approaches discussed are only a few of the many that are available to assist people in better managing their time. Individuals can accomplish their objectives, lower their stress levels, and lead more balanced lives by adopting these tools and approaches into their daily routine.

CHAPTER 4

Balancing Work and Life

Achieving a healthy balance between work and life requires setting boundaries in both areas. Without limits, it may be difficult to keep your personal and work lives separate, which could result in stress, burnout, and a poor quality of life.

Entrepreneurs often face unique challenges when it comes to balancing work and life. With the demands of starting and running a business, it can be challenging to find time for personal activities, hobbies, and family or social life.

Importance of Balancing Work and Life

Balancing work and life is crucial for overall well-being and happiness. Here are some reasons why it's important:

Reduced stress: When work and personal life are out of balance, it can lead to stress and burnout. High levels of stress can negatively impact your physical and mental health, as well as your relationships and overall quality of life. By finding a healthy balance between work and personal life, you can reduce stress and increase your overall well-being. This can lead to better job performance, better relationships, and better overall health.

Improved productivity: Taking breaks and focusing on personal interests can help you recharge and improve your focus when you return to work. When you are energized and focused, you may find that you are more productive and efficient in your work. Additionally, finding a balance between work and personal life can help you avoid burnout, which can lead to decreased productivity and job satisfaction.

Stronger relationships: Prioritizing time with loved ones can help you build and maintain strong relationships. These relationships can provide a source of support and encouragement during difficult times. By finding a healthy balance between work and personal life, you can prioritize time with loved ones and improve the quality of your relationships.

Increased job satisfaction: When work and personal life are in balance, you may find that you are more satisfied with both areas of your life. This can lead to increased job satisfaction and overall happiness. By prioritizing self-care and personal interests, you may find that you are more fulfilled and engaged in both areas of your life.

Better physical and mental health: Taking care of your physical and mental health is essential for overall well-being. When work and personal life are out of balance, it can be difficult to find time for self-care and prioritize your health. By finding a healthy balance between work and personal life, you can prioritize self-care and reduce the risk of health issues related to stress and burnout. This can lead to better physical and mental health, which can improve your overall quality of life.

Setting Boundaries for Work and Personal Time

Setting boundaries for work and personal life is important for achieving a healthy balance between the two. Here are some tips for setting effective boundaries:

1. Establish clear work hours: Determine what your work hours will be and communicate them to your colleagues and clients. This will help you avoid feeling like you need to be available at all times and will allow you to establish a clear separation between work and personal time

2. Avoid checking work emails and messages during personal time: Unless it's an emergency, try to avoid checking work emails and messages during personal time. Set clear expectations with colleagues and clients about when you will be available and when you will not. If you do need to check messages during personal time, set a time limit and stick to it.

3. Practice mindfulness: Incorporating mindfulness practices into your daily routine can help you stay focused and reduce stress. Consider meditation, deep breathing exercises, or a gratitude journal to help you start your day on a positive note. Even taking a few minutes to check in

with yourself throughout the day can help you stay centered and calm.

4. Set boundaries with clients or customers: It's important to be clear with your clients or customers about your availability and response times. Setting expectations for communication can help you avoid feeling like you're "always on" and allow you to better manage your personal time. Consider setting specific hours when you are available for calls or emails, and avoid taking work-related calls or emails during personal time.

5. Prioritize self-care: Taking care of your physical and mental health is essential to achieving a healthy work-life balance. This means getting enough sleep, eating a healthy diet, and engaging in regular exercise. It's also important to take breaks throughout the day to stretch or take a walk, and to make time for activities that bring you joy, such as hobbies or creative pursuits.

6. Make time for relationships: Building and maintaining strong relationships with friends, family, or a significant other can provide a source of support and encouragement outside of work. Schedule regular time to connect with loved ones, even if it's just a quick phone call or text message. Additionally, consider joining social groups or

clubs that align with your interests and provide an opportunity to meet new people.

7. Identify work-life integration opportunities: Look for opportunities to integrate work and personal life, such as attending industry conferences or networking events that also offer personal development opportunities. By combining work and personal interests, you can reduce stress and improve your overall satisfaction with both areas of your life.

8. Embrace flexibility: Embracing flexibility in your work schedule or location can help you better manage personal commitments and reduce stress. Consider working from home a few days a week or setting flexible hours that allow you to attend to personal commitments. Just be sure to communicate your schedule and availability with your team or clients to avoid any confusion.

Balancing work and life requires a holistic approach that considers your physical and mental well-being, relationships, and personal goals. By incorporating mindfulness practices, setting boundaries, prioritizing self-care, making time for relationships, identifying integration opportunities, and embracing flexibility, you can achieve a fulfilling and successful work-life balance.

Prioritizing Self-Care

Prioritizing self-care is one of the most important things you can do for yourself. Any deliberate action that promotes one's physical, mental, or emotional wellbeing is referred to as self-care. Self-care is important for maintaining a healthy work-life balance and general well-being, yet it is often overlooked.

Self-care goes beyond treating yourself to a spa day or other forms of pampering (although that can certainly be a part of it). It involves accepting responsibility for your own health and realizing the value of caring yourself. You are investing in your own physical, emotional, and mental wellness when you prioritize self-care.

Time is one of the largest barriers to self-care. Many people believe they don't have enough time to engage in self-care activities. Self-care does not, however, have to take up much time. By implementing basic self-care routines into your daily schedule, you can start small. You may, for instance, spend a few minutes each day engaging in deep breathing exercises or meditation, or you could go for a brief stroll around the block during your lunch break.

Guilt is another barrier to self-care. Many people feel guilty about taking time for themselves, especially if they feel overwhelmed by their obligations or that they ought to be working. Yet it's important to remember that taking good care of yourself is not being selfish. Taking care of yourself actually increases productivity and equips you with the tools you need to face daily obstacles.

It's also important to keep in mind that everyone's definition of self-care is different. One person's solution might not be suitable for another. Finding self-care rituals that speak to you and make you feel good is the key. Running or participating in sports may be preferred by some people as a great way to relieve stress, while others may find yoga or meditation to be very helpful.

Finally, it's important to recognize that self-care is a continuous process. You can't just do it once and put it out of your mind. Instead, it is a daily practice that demands continued focus and dedication. The commitment you make to your own wellbeing when you prioritize self-care will benefit you in countless ways.

Prioritizing self-care is essential for maintaining a healthy work-life balance and overall well-being. By taking small steps to care for yourself physically, mentally, and emotionally, you can reduce stress, improve your mood, and enhance your overall quality of life. Remember that self-care is not selfish, and that it's an ongoing practice that requires ongoing attention and commitment. With these strategies in place, you can prioritize self-care and enjoy a happier, healthier life.

Here are some tips for prioritizing self-care:

1. Exercise regularly: Exercise has numerous physical and mental health benefits. It can improve your mood, reduce stress, and boost your energy levels. Try to make time for exercise at least a few times per week. This could be as simple as going for a walk, doing yoga, or lifting weights.

2. Get enough sleep: Getting enough sleep is essential for maintaining good physical and mental health. Aim for at least seven to eight hours of sleep per night, and establish a consistent sleep schedule. Try to avoid using electronic devices before bedtime, and create a relaxing bedtime routine to help you wind down.

3. Eat a healthy diet: Eating a healthy diet can help you feel better physically and mentally. Try to eat a balanced diet that includes plenty of fruits, vegetables, whole grains, and lean protein. Limit your intake of processed foods, sugary drinks, and alcohol.

4. Take breaks: It's important to take breaks throughout the day to recharge your batteries. This could mean taking a walk outside, chatting with a friend, or simply taking a few

deep breaths. Taking breaks can help you avoid burnout and improve your overall productivity.

5. Prioritize social connections: Social connections are important for mental and emotional well-being. Make time for friends and family, and participate in social activities that you enjoy. This could be as simple as having a weekly phone call with a friend or joining a club or group that interests you.

Self-care is not selfish; rather, it is a necessary habit for living a happy and healthy life. It is significant to remember that everyone's definition of self-care is different, and what works for one person might not work for another. It's crucial to pay attention to your body and figure out what activities improve your general wellbeing. Making self-care a priority can also make you more successful, innovative, and productive in both your personal and professional lives.

CHAPTER 5

Overcoming Procrastination and Boosting Productivity

Procrastination is the act of delaying or postponing a task or decision, usually until a later time or date. It is a habit that many people practice in often, and it can be harmful to one's success and productivity. In any area of life, from personal to professional, procrastination can result in stress, anxiety, and low self-esteem.

There are various causes of procrastination. Some people put off doing anything because they are unsure of where to start and feel overwhelmed by the task at hand. Some people put things off till the last minute because they think they perform best under pressure. Others delay because they worry about succeeding or failing.

Procrastination can have negative effects regardless of the reasons. It may result in missed deadlines, poor work, and lost opportunities. Stress, anxiety, and other negative emotions that might have an effect on one's mental health and wellbeing can result from procrastination.

Understanding why procrastination happens and creating management solutions are crucial for overcoming it. One strategy is to divide difficult activities into smaller, easier-to-manage ones. Making progress and experiencing a sense of accomplishment in this way can help one gain momentum and motivation. Setting deadlines and holding oneself responsible for reaching them is an alternative strategy. This can contribute to a sense of urgency and reduce the likelihood that one will put anything off.

It is also important to identify and address the underlying causes of procrastination. For example, if procrastination is due to fear of failure, it may be helpful to challenge negative self-talk and practice self-compassion. If procrastination is due to feeling overwhelmed, it may be helpful to prioritize tasks and ask for help when needed.

Procrastination is a common habit that can have a negative impact on productivity and well-being. Individuals can overcome procrastination and achieve their goals by understanding why it occurs and developing strategies to manage it.

Strategies for Overcoming Procrastination

Procrastination is a common challenge that many people face. Overcoming procrastination requires a combination of understanding the reasons behind it and developing strategies to manage it. Here are some strategies for overcoming procrastination:

1. Creating a schedule: Scheduling your day or week can help you stay focused and on track. It gives you a clear plan of what you need to accomplish and when. You can use a planner or calendar to schedule your tasks and activities, and be sure to include breaks or downtime to help prevent burnout.

2. Using a timer: The Pomodoro Technique is a popular time management technique that involves setting a timer for 25 minutes and working on a task until the timer goes off. Then, you take a short break and repeat the process. This can help you stay focused and productive, and also gives you regular breaks to help prevent burnout.

3. Eliminating distractions: Distractions can be a major source of procrastination, so it's important to identify and eliminate them. This could include turning off your phone, closing social media tabs, or working in a quiet space.

4. Getting an accountability partner: Having someone else hold you accountable can be a powerful motivator. Share your goals and progress with someone you trust, and ask them to check in with you regularly to make sure you're making progress.

5. Practicing self-compassion: Procrastination can be frustrating, but it's important to be kind to yourself and practice self-compassion. Remember that everyone struggles with procrastination at times, and it's okay to make mistakes or not be perfect. Treat yourself with the same kindness and understanding you would offer a friend.

Overall, overcoming procrastination is about finding strategies and techniques that work for you. Experiment with different approaches until you find what works best for your unique situation and challenges. With practice and persistence, you can develop habits that help you overcome procrastination and achieve your goals.

Tips for Boosting Productivity

Boosting productivity is a key factor in achieving success, both in your personal and professional life. It involves maximizing your efficiency, managing your time effectively, and producing high-quality work. Improving your productivity can help you achieve your goals faster, reduce stress, and increase your overall satisfaction with your work. Whether you're a student, employee, or entrepreneur, there are many strategies you can use to boost your productivity and achieve your goals. Let's explore some unique and effective tips for increasing productivity and achieving success.

1. Use music to boost your mood and energy: Listening to music while you work can help you stay focused, block out distractions, and increase your energy levels. Research shows that music can also help improve your mood and reduce stress, leading to increased productivity. Try creating a playlist of instrumental music or music without lyrics to avoid getting distracted.

2. Try a standing desk: Sitting for long periods of time can lead to decreased productivity and fatigue. Using a standing desk can help improve posture, increase energy levels, and boost productivity. A standing desk can also help reduce

the risk of certain health problems associated with sitting for long periods.

3. Use aromatherapy: Essential oils like lavender, peppermint, and lemon can help improve focus, reduce stress, and boost productivity. Aromatherapy works by stimulating the olfactory senses, which can help improve mood and cognitive function. Use a diffuser or apply essential oils topically to experience their benefits.

4. Take a power nap: A short nap can help you recharge and increase productivity. Power naps can help reduce fatigue, improve mood, and increase cognitive function. Set an alarm for 20-30 minutes to avoid oversleeping and disrupting your sleep cycle.

5. Incorporate exercise breaks: Exercise can help increase productivity by boosting energy levels, reducing stress, and improving focus. Incorporate short exercise breaks throughout the day to keep your energy levels up. This can include stretches, yoga, or a quick walk.

6. Get outside: Spending time in nature can help reduce stress and increase creativity and productivity. Taking a short walk outside during your breaks or working in a park or outdoor space can help improve your mood and cognitive function.

7. Practice gratitude: Gratitude can help improve your mood and increase productivity. Taking a few minutes each day to reflect on what you're thankful for can help improve your mental health and increase motivation.

8. Take on a new challenge: Challenging yourself with a new project or task can help increase motivation and creativity. Choose something that's slightly outside of your comfort zone and work on it in small increments each day. This can help you stay engaged and interested in your work, leading to increased productivity.

In conclusion, boosting productivity is an important aspect of achieving success in various areas of life. By implementing some of the tips discussed, such as setting using music and aromatherapy, and taking breaks, you can improve your efficiency, focus, and motivation. Remember that productivity is not just about working harder, but also about working smarter. It's important to find a balance between work and rest, and to take care of your physical and mental health in order to maintain a high level of productivity. With dedication, discipline, and the right mindset, you can increase your productivity and achieve your goals.

CHAPTER 6

Maintaining Your Time Management System

Maintaining a time management system is crucial for anyone who wants to be productive and achieve their goals. Without a proper system in place, it's easy to get overwhelmed, forget important tasks, and waste time on unproductive activities.

Maintaining a time management system can be challenging, but it's essential if you want to stay on top of your game. By having a structured approach to managing your time, you can ensure that you're spending your days in a productive and efficient manner, accomplishing the things that matter most to you.

Whether you're a busy professional, a student, or a stay-at-home parent, developing and maintaining a time management system can help you achieve your goals, reduce stress, and create more time for the things you love. With the right tools and techniques, you can take control of your time and make the most of every day.

Here are some tips for maintaining your time management system:

Review and update your system regularly: Your time management system should be a living document that evolves as your priorities and needs change. Set aside time at least once a week to review your system and make any necessary updates. This could involve adding new tasks, rearranging priorities, or reevaluating the time you've allocated to certain activities.

Stay organized: Make sure you have a dedicated space for your time management system. Whether you use a planner, a digital tool, or a combination of both, keep everything in one place so you can easily access it when you need it. Use color-coding or other organizational tools to make your system easy to navigate.

Be realistic: It's important to set achievable goals and allocate realistic amounts of time to each task. If you consistently find yourself falling behind or struggling to complete everything on your to-do list, you may need to adjust your expectations and be more selective about the tasks you take on.

Prioritize: Prioritization is key to effective time management. Make sure you're spending your time on the most important tasks, and avoid getting bogged down in unimportant or low-priority activities. Use tools like the Eisenhower matrix to help you prioritize your tasks based on their urgency and importance.

Stay focused: It's easy to get distracted by email, social media, and other interruptions throughout the day. To stay focused, try using time blocking or the Pomodoro technique to help you concentrate on your work for set periods of time. You can also use tools like website blockers or app timers to limit your access to distracting websites or apps during work hours.

Be flexible: Even with the best time management system, unexpected events can throw off your plans. Be prepared to adjust your schedule or priorities as needed, and don't be too hard on yourself if things don't always go according to plan.

By following these tips, you can create and maintain a time management system that helps you stay productive, focused, and on track to achieve your goals.

Reviewing Your Time Management System

Reviewing your time management system is a crucial step in maintaining an effective system. Regularly assessing how you are managing your time allows you to identify areas of improvement, make necessary adjustments, and ensure that you are on track to achieve your goals.

When reviewing your time management system, it's important to approach the process with an open mind and a willingness to make changes. The goal of the review process is to identify areas where you can improve your time management skills, eliminate distractions, and become more productive.

Some tips on how to review your time management system effectively:

1. Assess your goals: Take some time to think about your long-term goals and how your time management system is helping you achieve them. Are you making progress toward your goals, or do you need to change your strategy? Make use of your goals to help you identify areas where you need to make changes.

2. Examine your tools: Consider the time management tools and techniques you employ. Are they assisting you in remaining organized and focused, or are they causing additional distractions? Determine which tools are effective for you and which need to be modified or eliminated.

3. Identify your strengths and weaknesses: Take an honest look at your time management strengths and weaknesses. Are you prone to procrastination or easily distracted? You can develop strategies to overcome your weaknesses once you've identified them.

4. Look for patterns: Review your calendar or to-do list for any patterns or trends in how you spend your time. Is there a time of day when you are most productive, or are there activities that always take longer than expected? Look for patterns that will help you adjust your strategy.

5. Hold yourself accountable for implementing the changes you make to your time management system. Keep track of your progress, rejoice in your victories, and be honest with yourself about any setbacks or difficulties.

CONCLUSION

Time Management for Entrepreneurs provides valuable insights and practical tips for entrepreneurs who struggle with managing their time effectively. This book emphasizes the importance of setting clear goals, prioritizing tasks, and delegating responsibilities to achieve success in business. It also highlights the significance of taking breaks and avoiding burnout, as well as the benefits of adopting a positive mindset and a growth-oriented approach.

Throughout this book, the author emphasizes the importance of being intentional and disciplined when managing time, as time is a valuable resource that cannot be replaced once lost. Entrepreneurs can boost their productivity, reduce stress, and achieve a better work-life balance by implementing the strategies outlined in this book.

Time Management for Entrepreneurs is a great resource for anyone who wants to improve their time management abilities. This book is well-written and simple to read, with numerous real-life examples and case studies to illustrate key concepts. The book's practical tips and techniques are applicable to a wide range of industries and professions.